THE CHANGING WORLD OF RETIREMENT PLANNING

WORKBOOK 2

Place label here. Include:

Instructor name(s)

FINRA member firm

Broker-dealer disclosure

THE CHANGING WORLD OF RETIREMENT PLANNING

Typesetting by *Wordzworth.com*

Contents

Protecting Against Market Loss

Retirement Distribution Pitfalls

Long-Term Care Planning

Appendix 1:   Risk Profile Questionnaire

SECTION SIX

Protecting Against Market Loss

Introduction

When there is volatility in the stock market retirees are confronted with the difficult question of how to grow their money productively while safeguarding against downturns from which they may not recover. How do you outdistance inflation and ensure that your assets stretch the length of your retirement while mitigating dramatic market loss? How you answer these questions may be the difference between running out of money too soon and living a prosperous retirement.

In this section we will discuss the following:

- The impact of dramatic market loss on your retirement portfolio

- Is "buy and hold" an appropriate strategy for retirement?

- Is "asset allocation" alone enough to protect your portfolio?

- How to mitigate two types of investment risk to achieve true portfolio diversification

The Old Paradigm

The "old" paradigm as it relates to stock market investing is as follows:

- The stock market will always vindicate itself

- "Buy and hold" is an appropriate long-term investment strategy during retirement

- Diversifying your portfolio through proper asset allocation will protect your retirement against dramatic swings in the stock market

The New Paradigm

The "new" paradigm states that retirees have to approach stock market volatility during retirement in a whole new light:

- The market is more unpredictable and volatile than ever

- Buy and hold strategies may be incompatible with volatile markets

- Asset allocation is no longer enough to protect against all the risks your portfolio may face

- A down market at the wrong time may force you to postpone retirement indefinitely[1]

[1] Investments are not guaranteed and are subject to investment risk including the possible loss of principal. The investment return and principal value of the security will fluctuate so that when redeemed, may be worth more or less than the original investment.

Is Your Portfolio Truly Diversified?

Portfolio diversification is a strategy that has been utilized by investors for decades. Will the traditional approach to portfolio diversification be enough to safeguard your portfolio in retirement?

- In 2008 many investors lost between 30 and 50%[2]

- How did that happen when most of these investors had *diversified* portfolios?

- True diversification only takes place when investors protect themselves against all of the investment risks that lead to market loss

[2] Yahoo Finance

There are Two Types of Investment Risk

Investment Risk #1: Unsystematic Risk

- **Definition**: The investment risk associated with investing in a single company[3]

- **Example**: employees go on strike, CEO dies, product failure, scandal, poor management, mal-investment, etc.

Case Study:

What would have happened if you had invested your entire retirement portfolio in a company called Citigroup (C) back in 2007?[4] Over the course of a single year, Citigroup stock crashed and became almost worthless. This came about because of mal-investment in credit default swaps and derivatives.

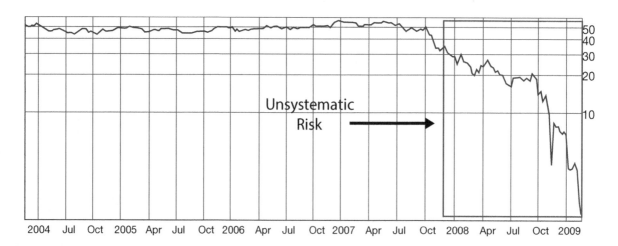

3 Investopedia.com

4 Investments are not guaranteed and are subject to investment risk including the possible loss of principal. The investment return and principal value of the security will fluctuate so that when redeemed, may be worth more or less than the original investment.

Solution to Unsystematic Risk: Asset Allocation

To mitigate unsystematic risk, don't put all your eggs in one basket. This is accomplished through *asset allocation*.[5]

Definition: Investing in a broad range of companies and sectors in an effort to decrease risk and increase return while accounting for individual investor risk tolerance and financial objectives.[6]

Asset Allocation[7]

Cash	18.86%
US Stocks	38.34%
Non-US Stocks	15.31%
Bonds	27.08%
Other	0.41%
Total	100%

The above chart shows an example of asset allocation. This particular portfolio has money spread between asset classes (US Stocks, Non-US Stocks, Bonds, etc.) and sectors (manufacturing, information, service).[8]

---

[5] Using diversification/asset allocation as part of your investment strategy neither assures nor guarantees better performance and cannot protect against loss in declining markets

[6] Investopedia.com

[7] The hypothetical example is for illustrative purposes only and each individual's situation is different

[8] Morningstar

To mitigate a risk like Citigroup (C), this portfolio only had a fraction of its overall holdings (16.97%) in the financial sector, only a small portion of which may have been invested in Citigroup. Even though Citigroup's stock price fell dramatically, the other companies in that sector were able to buoy up the overall portfolio.

Sector	Portfolio %
Information	16.3
Software	2.19
Hardware	7.4
Media	1.33
Telecom	5.38
Service Economy	40.58
Healthcare	11.88
Consumer Services	5.89
Business Services	5.84
Financial Services	16.97
Manufacturing Economy	43.07
Consumer Goods	13.01
Industrial Materials	16.07
Energy	9.07
Utilities	4.93
Not Classified	0.04

Citigroup (C)

Investment Risk #2: Systematic Risk

Is asset allocation enough to protect your portfolio from dramatic downturns in the market? Not without taking steps to protect against Investment Risk #2, systematic risk.

- **Definition:** The risk inherent to the entire market or the entire economic system[9]

- **Example:** war, 9/11, inflation, higher taxes, credit crises, recessions, depressions, etc.

It is important to note that no amount of diversification or asset allocation can protect you against systematic risk!

[9] Investopedia.com

The Dangers of Systematic Risk

To understand the perils of systematic risk, let's take a look at the performance of a well "diversified" stock portfolio from 2004 to 2009.[10]

Stock Portfolio

- 25% invested in Russell 2000 Index[11]

- 25% invested in Dow Jones Industrial Index[12]

- 25% invested in NASDAQ Index[13]

- 25% invested in S&P 500 Index[14]

Total Representation: 2,630 companies

Is this *true* diversification?

Let's take a look at what each individual index did during that five year period from 2004 to 2009:[15]

---

[10] This is a hypothetical example for illustrative purposes and does not reference any specific client experience. Indices are not managed and do not incur fees or expenses. It is not possible to invest directly in an index

[11] The Russell 2000 index is an index measuring the performance of approximately 2,000 small-cap companies in the Russell 3000 Index, which is made up of 3,000 of the biggest U.S. stocks. The Russell 2000 serves as a benchmark for small-cap stocks in the United States

[12] The Dow Jones Industrial Index is a price-weighted average of 30 significant stocks traded on the New York Stock Exchange (NYSE) and the NASDAQ

[13] The NASDAQ Index is a stock market index of the common stocks and similar securities (e.g. ADRs, tracking stocks, limited partnership interests) listed on the NASDAQ stock market

[14] The Standard & Poor's 500 Index (S&P 500) is an index of 500 stocks seen as a leading indicator of U.S. equities and a reflection of the performance of the large cap universe, made up of companies selected by economists

[15] Yahoo Finance

Russell 2000: 2004-2009

Past performance is not indicative of future results. Indices are not managed and do not incur fees or expenses. It is not possible to invest directly in an index

Dow Jones: 2004-2009

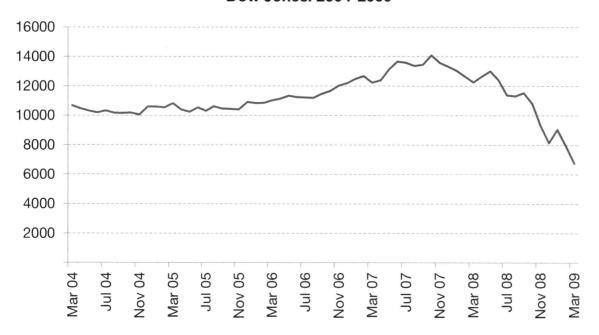

Past performance is not indicative of future results. Indices are not managed and do not incur fees or expenses. It is not possible to invest directly in an index.

NASDAQ: 2004-2009

Past performance is not indicative of future results. Indices are not managed and do not incur fees or expenses. It is not possible to invest directly in an index.

S&P 500: 2004-2009

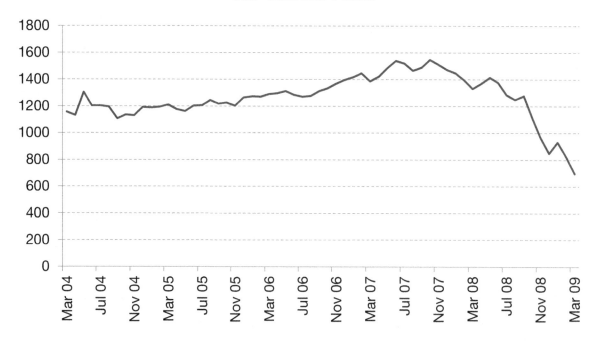

Past performance is not indicative of future results. Indices are not managed and do not incur fees or expenses. It is not possible to invest directly in an index.

Now that we've seen how each one of these individual indices faired over that 5 year time frame, let's overlap them in a single chart to get a sense for how they behaved with respect to each other.

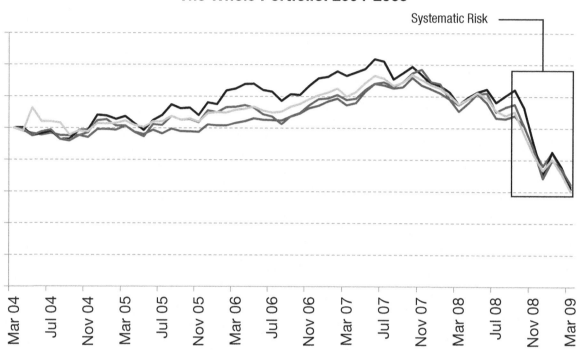

The Whole Portfolio: 2004-2009

Systematic Risk

Past performance is not indicative of future results. Indices are not managed and do not incur fees or expenses. It is not possible to invest directly in an index.

By overlapping these charts, it's clear that all of these indices seem to be taking their cues from the same market forces. In fact, when the market dropped dramatically in 2008, all 2,630 companies dropped at the same time and in dramatic fashion. This chart exposes the perils of systematic risk. How did your portfolio do in 2008?

As we can see, asset allocation alone was completely ineffective at preventing catastrophic loss in a "well-diversified" stock portfolio.

Solution to Systematic Risk: Principal Protection Program

So how do we manage systematic risk? One way to mitigate systematic risk is to consider incorporating a Principal Protection Program such as a Fixed Indexed Annuity.[16]

A Fixed Indexed Annuity can be defined as follows:

Definition: An annuity that allows you to off-load systematic risk to a large financial institution. Such programs link the growth of your portfolio to the upward movement of a stock market index without exposure to market loss.[17]

Fixed Indexed Annuities are Insurance Contracts and do not directly participate in any stock, bond or equity investments. You are not buying any shares of Stocks, bonds or shares of an index. The Market index value does not include the dividends paid on the underlying market index. These dividends are also not reflected in any indexed

---

[16] The tax-deferred feature of an annuity should not be a factor in purchasing an annuity in a tax-qualified plan. Tax deferral is provided by the plan and the tax-deferral of the annuity does not provide any additional benefit. Annuities are subject to additional fees and expenses to which other tax-qualified funding vehicles may not be subject. Individuals should only purchase an annuity in a qualified plan when its other benefits, such as lifetime income payments, family protection through death benefits, and/or guaranteed fees meet their current needs.

Annuities have limitations. They are long-term vehicles designed for retirement purposes. They are not intended to replace emergency funds, to be used as income for day-to-day expenses, or to fund short-term savings goals. Investing involves risk.

A fixed indexed annuity is not a stock market investment and does not directly participate in any stock or equity investment. It may be appropriate for individuals who want guaranteed interest rates and the potential for lifetime income. Guarantees are subject to the claims-paying ability of the issuing insurance company.

Lifetime income may be provided through the purchase of an optional rider for an additional cost or through annuitization at no additional cost. If you take withdrawals before you're age 59½, you may have to pay a 10% early withdrawal federal tax penalty in addition to ordinary income taxes. Withdrawals may trigger early surrender charges, reduce your death benefit and contract value.

Not a deposit • Not FDIC or NCUSIF insured • Not guaranteed by the institution • Not insured by any federal government agency • May lose value

The guarantee of the annuity is backed by the claims paying ability of the issuing insurance company. Although it is possible to have guaranteed income for life with a fixed annuity, there is no assurance that this income will keep up with inflation.

[17] The hypothetical example is for illustrative purposes only. Consult with your tax and legal advisors regarding your individual situation.

interest that may be credited to your contact. Such contracts have substantial variation in terms, costs of guarantees and features and may cap participation or returns in significant ways. Investors are cautioned to carefully review a fixed index annuity for its features, costs, and risk and how the variables are calculated. Any guarantees are backed by the financial strength of the insurance company.

Why does it make sense to protect your principal?

With all of the uncertainties in the world, how can you protect your retirement assets from dramatic market fluctuation at a period in your life when you can least afford to lose money?

First, let's look at some statistical probabilities of various events occurring in the arc of an average year's time.

Compare the ownership of protection with the likelihood of an event occurring that will require that protection. What's the probability of becoming disabled or needing nursing care and what's the probability that you will be protected in those instances?

Family Risks to Family per Year [18]

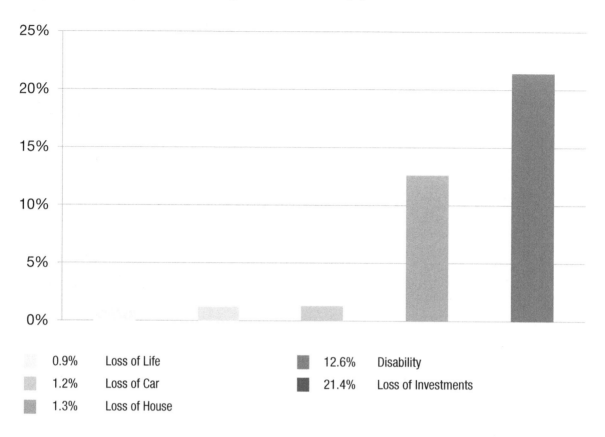

0.9%	Loss of Life	
1.2%	Loss of Car	
1.3%	Loss of House	
12.6%	Disability	
21.4%	Loss of Investments	

Ironically, it appears that the higher the probability of something happening, the less likely there are measures in place to protect against it.

Even more surprising is the low likelihood that we might protect our retirement assets despite the fact that the S&P 500 has declined 13 times in the last 54 years or, roughly, once every five years.

[18] 2001 CSO Table; U.S. Department of Transportation – Traffic Safety Facts www.nhtsa.gov; National Fire Protection Association 2013 report; Cornell University 2012 Disability Status Report; Standard & Poor's Index Services (1953-2015)

Rebuilding—How Long Will It Take?

How long does it take to break even after a large financial loss in your portfolio? [19]

Portfolio is Down	Total Return Needed to Break Even	Years to Break Even Assuming a Return of...				
		3%	5%	8%	10%	12%
10%	11%	3.6	2.2	1.4	1.1	0.9
20%	25%	7.5	4.6	2.9	2.3	2.0
30%	43%	12.1	7.3	4.6	3.7	3.1
40%	67%	17.3	10.5	6.6	5.4	4.5
50%	100%	23.4	14.2	9.0	7.3	6.1
60%	150%	31.0	18.8	11.9	9.6	8.1
70%	233%	40.7	24.7	15.6	12.6	10.6
80%	400%	54.4	33.0	20.9	16.9	14.2
90%	900%	77.9	47.2	29.9	24.2	20.3

The above chart shows how long it would take to recover from just one down year. For example, if your portfolio went down 40%, you would need to get 67% just to break even. At 8% growth, it would take 6.6 years for you to get back to square one.[20]

[19] Van Kampen Investments
[20] The Hypothetical example is for illustrative purposes only and each individual's situation is different

Three Ways to Diversify Your Money

So far we've talked about the two basic types of investment risk that threaten your portfolio. Now we'll discuss the three basic ways to diversify your money in an attempt to mitigate those risks:

1. Emergency Fund

2. Asset Allocation[21]

3. Principal Protection Program

Let's take a look at each one of these one by one.

Emergency Fund

- No more than 6 months' worth of income

- Very liquid

- Low returns, typically between 0 and 2%

- Part of the "Taxable Bucket"

---

[21] Using diversification/asset allocation as part of your investment strategy neither assures nor guarantees better performance and cannot protect against loss in declining markets.

Because of its tax-inefficiency, we have to be sure that we only hold a prescribed amount of money in this bucket. If you amortize the tax inefficiencies of this bucket out over a 35 year retirement, you may end up paying hundreds of thousands of dollars in taxation that is largely avoidable.

Asset Allocation

Asset allocation is used to mitigate risk in the portion of your portfolio you are willing to watch rise and fall with the market. The following are a few guidelines regarding asset allocation:

- Contribute the percentage of your assets you're comfortable watching go up and down in the market
- Rule of Thumb: Take your age, subtract 100 and contribute to asset allocation
  - Example: A 60 year old might grow 40% of his assets in a well-diversified portfolio through asset allocation.[22]
- Asset allocation can take place in the taxable, tax-deferred or tax-advantaged buckets
- Typical rates of return range from -30% to +30%

Principal Protection Program

This program is typically utilized in the form of a Fixed Indexed Annuity (FIA). The guarantee of the annuity is backed by the claims paying ability of the issuing company. Although it is possible to have guaranteed income for life with a fixed annuity, there is no assurance that this income will keep up with inflation. These

[22] The hypothetical example is for illustrative purposes only. Consult with your tax and legal advisors regarding your individual situation.

annuities link the growth of your portfolio to the upward movement of a stock market index like the S&P 500, without exposure to market loss. As a trade-off for the guarantee, average rates of return will be lower than typical stock market returns. The following are a few guidelines relating to Principal Protection Programs:

- Contribute the portion of your assets you're not comfortable losing in the stock market

- Rule of Thumb: convert your age to a percentage, and that's how much you might allocate towards a Principal Protection Program

    - Example: A 60 year old might put 60% of their assets into a Principal Protection Program

- Moderately liquid

- Guarantees against loss

    - Guarantee is subject to the claims paying ability of the insurance company who is solely responsible for all obligations under its policies

- As a tradeoff for the guarantee, average rates of return will be lower than typical stock market returns

    - Average rates of return may range between 3% and 8%

- There may be a surrender charge imposed during the first 5 to 10 years that you own the contract.

- Withdrawals prior to age 59 ½ may result in a 10% federal tax penalty, in addition to any ordinary income tax.

In Summary

Traditional risk mitigation strategies may not be enough to protect your portfolio from dramatic market loss. In order to grow your money productively while safeguarding against downturns in the market, you might consider the following:

- There are two types of investment risks

- Unsystematic Risk: the risk a single stock could go down

  - Examples: uncompetitive products, death of a CEO, corporate malfeasance, etc.

  - Risk Mitigation: Asset Allocation

- Systematic Risk: the risk the entire market or "system" could go down

  - Examples: World War, 9/11, inflation, societal upheaval, collateralized debt obligations (2008)

  - Risk Mitigation: Principal Protection Program in the form of a Fixed Indexed Annuity (FIA)

Begin by asking yourself what portion of your portfolio you're comfortable watching rise and fall with the stock market. Allocate this portion to a well-balanced, properly asset-allocated portfolio. The remainder can be repositioned to a Principal Protection Program that allows you to participate in the upward movement of the stock market without exposure to market loss.

SECTION SEVEN

Retirement Distribution Pitfalls

Introduction

In this section we cover the primary mistakes people make when they begin to distribute their assets in retirement. We also cover some of the potential solutions.

There are 3 main retirement distribution pitfalls:

1. Withdrawing money too quickly

2. Liquidating your assets in the wrong order

3. Getting the wrong sequence of returns on your investments during the distribution phase

Pitfall #1: Rate of Withdrawal

In 1994 a financial advisor named William Bengen proposed "the 4% rule".[23] This rule has since been adopted by many retirement strategists. This rule says the following:

- You should not withdraw more than 4% of your retirement assets per year

- By exceeding this limit you increase the likelihood you will run out of money before you die

In addition to the 4% rule, there are a number of other variables you should consider when calculating your maximum distributions in a given year. These variable are as follows:

- Life expectancy

- Likely rates of return

- Asset mix of stocks vs. bonds

- Age at retirement

- Sequence of returns

By the end of this section, you should be able to evaluate whether the 4% rule still applies to you. Let's take a look at each of these variables one by one.

---

[23] http://www.nytimes.com/2013/05/15/business/retirementspecial/the-4-rule-for-retirement-withdrawals-may-be-outdated.html

Life expectancy

The younger you are at retirement, the lower the acceptable level of distributions. The longer you need your money to last, the more conservative the level of distributions. For example:

- If you retire at 70, you can likely withdraw 6 or 7% of your assets in a given year
- If you retire at 62, that number falls to as low as 2 or 3%[24]

The 4% rule can vary widely based on the year in which you decide to begin taking distributions from your retirement accounts. Other variables may include the following:

- When do you plan on retiring? How old will you be?
- Who long do you plan on living in retirement?
- What is your life expectancy?

Rates of Return

William Bengen's theory was predicated upon an assumed rate of return for both stocks and bonds:

- The average ROR predicted for stocks was 8% and bonds was 6.6%
- Today bonds average closer to 2.4%

In today's environment, a 4% withdrawal rate *may* be too aggressive.[25] We may not get the required rates of return in our stock and bond portfolios to justify taking distributions as large as 4%.

---

[24] The hypothetical example is used for illustrative purposes only and each individual's situation is different.
[25] http://www.investopedia.com/articles/personal-finance/120513/why-4-retirement-rule-no-longer-safe.asp

Asset Mix

The next variable, asset mix, has to do with the makeup of your portfolio. What percentage is stocks? What percentage is bonds? As you will see with the following examples, the less money you have in the stock market, the greater the likelihood you will run out of money before you die according to the 4% rule:

- 100% Bond Portfolio
  - 4% withdrawal rate
  - 35% chance money will last 30 years
- 75% Stock and 25% Bond Portfolio
  - 4% withdrawal rate
  - 100% chance money will last 30 years
- 6% withdrawal rate
  - 100% Bond Portfolio—11% chance of lasting 30 years
  - 75% Stocks and 25% Bonds—60% chance of lasting 30 years[26]

This last scenario shows the wisdom of the 4% rule. Statistically speaking, if you withdraw 6% from a portfolio with a 75/25 asset mix, you have a 60% likelihood of arriving safely at the end of your retirement.[27]

[26] http://www.forbes.com/sites/nextavenue/2013/06/10/how-much-to-withdraw-from-retirement-savings/

[27] Using diversification/asset allocation as part of your investment strategy neither assures nor guarantees better performance and cannot protect against loss in declining markets. The hypothetical example is for illustrative purposes only and each individual's situation is different

Withdrawal Rates: Other Variables

Other variables that should be considered when evaluating a safe rate at which to draw down your assets are the following:

- Tax rates

- Social Security Income

- Pensions

- Part-time work

- *Order of liquidation*

Pitfall #2: Order of Liquidation

The second great pitfall that can dramatically curtail the life of your retirement assets is "order of liquidation". First, let's define it:

- **Definition**: The order in which you spend down your assets in retirement

Spending assets down in the wrong order may dramatically affect how long your money lasts in retirement. By way of review, there are 3 basic types of accounts or "buckets" of money you can spend in retirement:

- Taxable bucket
- Tax-deferred bucket
- Tax-advantaged bucket

In what order should you liquidate these accounts in retirement? Taxable assets first? Then tax-deferred? The only way to truly determine the right order of liquidation is to utilize financial planning software that has algorithms that help figure it out. This software runs every possible liquidation order that is mathematically conceivable. After performing these calculations, it then tells you the order of liquidation that will maximize your cash flow in retirement. The difference in orders of liquidation can sometimes stretch into the millions of dollars!

Example

Here's an example to give real-life application to this concept:

- John and Sally, age 65
- Assets:
  - $200,000 in Mutual Funds at 6.5% (taxable)
  - $200,000 in CDs at 1% (taxable)
  - $600,000 in IRAs at 6.5% (tax-deferred)
  - $200,000 in Roth IRAs at 6.5% (tax-advantaged)
  - $200,000 in Stocks at 6.5% (taxable)
  - $100,000 in Non-Qualified Annuity at 6.5% (tax-deferred)
- Social Security: $30,000 per year inflated at 3%
- Lifestyle need: $80,000 per year after tax inflated at 3%
- 25% effective tax rate[28]

Order of Liquidation: Strategy #1

In our first strategy, we are going to distribute John and Sally's assets randomly in the following order:

1. Roth IRA
2. Stocks
3. Non-Qualified Annuity
4. Mutual Funds
5. IRA
6. CDs

---

[28] This example is for illustrative purposes only and is not a solicitation or recommendation of any investment strategy of product.

By doing so, John and Sally will be able to distribute $4,299,880 after tax over the course of their retirement. There's only one problem: they run out of money at age 93.

Order of Liquidation: Strategy #2

In this example, the computer software performs a series of algorithms that evaluates every possible liquidation order, then gives us the one that will allow John and Sally to distribute the most money over the course of their retirement. In this case, the computer determined that the best order of liquidation was as follows:

1. CDs
2. Stocks
3. Mutual Funds
4. Roth IRA
5. Non-Qualified Annuity
6. IRA

The following chart shows the benefits of liquidating your assets in the correct order:

Net Worth (After Providing Required Cash Flow)[29]

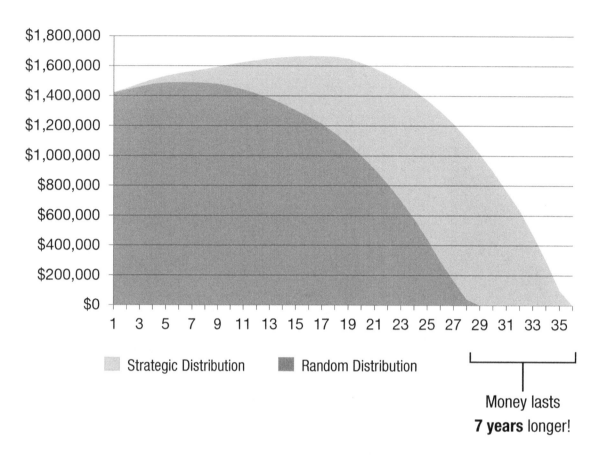

As you can see in the comparison, the most efficient order of liquidation extends the life of John and Sally's investments by 7 years! Remember, any strategy that extends the life of your retirement assets, whether by eliminating the taxation on your Social Security, or changing the order of liquidation of your investments in retirement, is something you should consider adopting.

[29] Insmark.com

In the chart below, we can see the dramatic increase in cash flow that can be directly attributed to changing the order of liquidation.

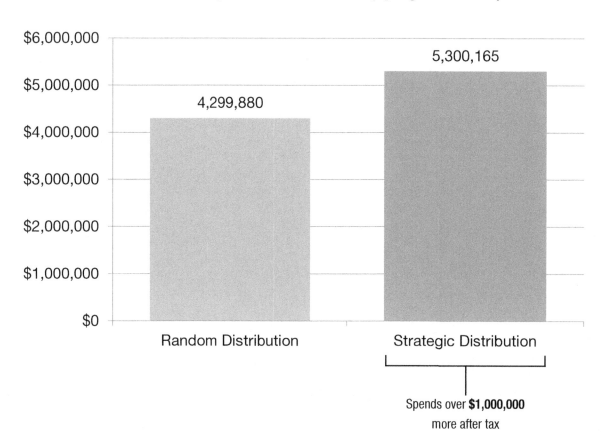

Cumulative Spendable Cash Flow (by Ages 100/100)[30]

- Random Distribution: 4,299,880
- Strategic Distribution: 5,300,165

Spends over **$1,000,000** more after tax

By utilizing algorithms that evaluate every possible order of liquidation, John and Sally were able to create a distribution plan that distributed an additional $1,000,000 of after tax income in retirement!

[30] Insmark.com

Pitfall #3: Sequence of Returns

The 3rd pitfall is getting the wrong sequence of returns in retirement. Let's begin by defining "sequence of returns":

- **Definition**: The order of investment returns in your portfolio.

The order in which you experience investment returns in retirement is critical to the sustainability of your retirement plan. The following factors should be considered when evaluating how to mitigate sequence of returns risk:

- You risk running out of money too soon if negative returns happen in the early years of retirement
- There is less inherent risk to your portfolio if those negative returns happen later in retirement
- Poor returns early on when coupled with withdrawals can dramatically reduce the life of your retirement assets

To illustrate the perils of "sequence of return" risk, consider the following example:[31]

- Two couples retire at the same time
- Both are age 65
- Both have $500,000

---

[31] The hypothetical example is for illustrative purposes only and each individual's situation is different.

- Both begin to withdraw 5% per year, adjusted for inflation at 3%

- Both average a net return of 6% per year

- Tom and Mary experience negative returns early in retirement, and positive returns later.

- Mike and Susan experience positive returns early in retirement, and negative returns later

Keep in mind, both couples are getting the exact same average rate of return on their investments. But because Tom and Mary experienced negative returns while taking distributions in the first three years of retirement, they ran out of money after only 13 years.

Mike and Susan, conversely, experienced nothing but positive returns in their early retirement years. Their average rate of return, like Tom and Mary, is 6%, but the negative returns didn't come until much later in their retirement. Because they experienced positive years early on, and negative years later on, they spent an extra $822,422 over the life of their retirement. Their money lasted 18 years longer even though they got the exact same average rate of return!

TOM AND MARY				MIKE AND SUSAN		
Sequence of returns: Poor, then strong				Sequence of returns: Strong, then poor		
Hypothetical				Hypothetical		
Net Return	Withdrawal	Balance	AGE	Net Return	Withdrawal	Balance
		$500,000	65			$500,000
-27.1	25,000	346,275	66	26.7	25,000	601,825
-16.5	25,750	267,638	67	10.1	25,750	634,259
-1.9	26,523	236,535	68	4.3	26,523	633,869
3.1	27,318	215,702	69	8.9	27,318	660,534
10.9	28,138	208,009	70	17.6	28,138	743,697
-9.4	28,982	162,199	71	22.5	28,982	875,527
7.4	29,851	142,141	72	-3.7	29,851	814,385
8.1	30,747	120,417	73	18.1	30,747	925,477
15.4	31,669	102,415	74	-6.1	31,669	839,286
9.4	32,619	76,356	75	9.2	32,619	880,880
6.2	33,598	45,410	76	7.6	33,598	911,675
12.4	34,606	12,143	77	9.6	34,606	961,268
2.8	12,143	0	78	22.4	35,644	1,132,964
11.4	-	-	79	-11	36,713	975,663
9	-	-	80	24.3	37,815	1,165,745
24.3	-	-	81	9	38,949	1,228,207
-11	-	-	82	11.4	40,118	1,323,532
22.4	-	-	83	2.8	41,321	1,318,113
9.6	-	-	84	12.4	42,561	1,433,720
7.6	-	-	85	6.2	43,838	1,476,055
9.2	-	-	86	9.4	45,153	1,565,407
-6.1	-	-	87	15.4	46,507	1,752,811
18.1	-	-	88	8.1	47,903	1,843,006
-3.7	-	-	89	7.4	49,340	1,926,397
22.5	-	-	90	-9.4	50,820	1,699,273
17.6	-	-	91	10.9	52,344	1,826,444
8.9	-	-	92	3.1	53,915	1,827,478
4.3	-	-	93	-1.9	55,532	1,738,278
10.1	-	-	94	-16.5	57,198	1,403,702
26.7	-	-	95	-27.1	58,914	980,350
Average Annual Net Return 6%				Average Annual Net Return 6%		

[32] https://www.securian.com/public/Securian/Documents/Retirement%20GPS/F69939-3.pdf

Because you can never predict the sequence in which you'll experience rates of return, sequence of returns risk is one that's worth paying attention to.

Sequence of Returns Risk: Potential Solution

So, how can you mitigate the potentially devastating impact of sequence of returns risk? The following is one potential solution:

- Reallocate a portion of your retirement savings to a Principal Protection Program in the form of a Fixed Indexed Annuity

- This protects your assets from exposure to market loss in your early years of retirement while still allowing you to participate in the upside of the stock market

- It allows you to benefit from the periods of higher returns in later retirement years.

In Summary

During this section we learned about the 3 basic retirement pitfalls that may cause you to run out of money sooner than anticipated:

- Retirement Distribution Pitfall #1: Rate of Withdrawal

    - By withdrawing too much, too soon, you may outlive your assets

    - Solution: never withdraw more than 4% of your assets, and perhaps less

- Retirement Distribution Pitfall #2: Order of Liquidation Risk

    - By liquidating your assets in the wrong order, you may prematurely deplete your retirement assets

    - Solution: Use computer software to determine the appropriate order of liquidation

- Retirement Distribution Pitfall #3: Sequence of Returns Risk

    - If you experience negative returns in your early retirement years while taking withdrawals, your portfolio may not recover

    - Solution: Allocate a portion of your retirement to a Principal Protection Program in the form of a Fixed Indexed Annuity.

SECTION EIGHT

Long-Term Care Planning

Introduction

An untimely long-term care event during retirement may unravel many of the benefits brought about by the strategies we've discussed to this point.

In this section, we will discuss:

- The effect long-term care may have on your retirement

- Medicaid spend-down rules

- "Community Spouse" rules

- Four common alternatives to pay for long-term care

- Recent innovations in long-term care planning

The Old Paradigm

Let's begin by discussing the "Old Paradigm" when it comes to planning for a long-term care event:

- Medicare will pay for long-term care expenses

- Assets can be gifted away in order to qualify for Medicaid faster

- Children can take care of aging parents

- "I won't end up needing long-term care."

- There are only three ways to mitigate long-term care risks:

  - Self-insure

  - Rely on family members

  - Buy expensive long-term care insurance

The New Paradigm

The latest statistics go a long way towards debunking the traditional paradigms when it comes to long-term care:

- National average cost of long-term care is $6,753 to $7,543 per month

- 70% of retirees will need long-term care at some time in their retirement

- Medicare does not pay for long-term care

- Medicaid only steps in when you're broke!

- The Medicaid look-back period is now 60 months

- Long-term care can destroy a lifetime of savings before it reaches the next generation

- Children are often incapable or resentful of taking on long-term care duties

- Expensive long-term care insurance is no longer the only way to safeguard against a long-term care event[33]

Confronting the realities of long-term care requires a perspective that accounts for new legislative and statistical realities that are unique to the 21st century.

---

[33] http://www.longtermcarelink.net/eldercare/medicaid_long_term_care.htm

Medicaid Spend-down Rules

Before we discuss the role Medicaid may play in your efforts to pay for the cost of long-term care, it's important to understand how Medicaid is defined:

- **Definition**: A joint federal and state program that helps low-income individuals or families pay for the costs associated with long-term medical and custodial care, provided they qualify. Although largely funded by the federal government, Medicaid is run by the state where coverage may vary.

So, in essence, Medicaid is only available to people who meet certain qualifications, i.e., you can't afford to pay for the cost of long-term care on your own.

Asset Qualifications

- A nursing home patient is not allowed to have more than $2,400 worth of "countable assets"
- The "community spouse" living at home is allowed to keep a limited amount of "countable assets" to live on:
    - $120,900 of liquid assets
    - one house
    - one car

Income Qualifications

- Community spouse is allowed to keep a Minimum Monthly Maintenance Needs Allowance (MMMNA)

- MMMNA varies by state, but averages around $2,500 per month

For these reasons experts cite long-term care as one of the greatest threats to your retirement. Many couples save their entire lives only to see their entire estate decimated in the waning years of their life through long-term care spend-down.

How Will You Pay for Long-Term Care Expenses?

So, we recognize that LTC is a huge risk that needs to be mitigated, but how does one go about doing it? There are 4 common ways to pay for long-term care:

- Plan to pay the costs yourself

- Ask your family members to take care of you

- Purchase a traditional long-term care insurance policy

- Purchase a life insurance policy with long-term care features

Which one of these options is right for you? It depends largely upon your situation and your individual needs.

Traditional Long-Term Care Insurance

Let's begin by evaluating traditional long-term care insurance. The following are a few considerations when evaluating this option:

- Underwriting is based on morbidity, not mortality

  - Morbidity is the likelihood you will have a long-term care event

  - Mortality is the likelihood you will die

- Joint or back issues may disqualify applicants

- Insured must no longer be able to perform 2 of 6 activities of daily living

  - Eating

  - Bathing

  - Dressing

  - Toileting

  - Transferring (walking)

  - Continence

- Premiums are not guaranteed and may rise

- Coverage is typically use-it-or-lose-it

- Expenses paid through reimbursement

  - Insured pays for coverage out of own pocket

  - Submits receipts to long-term care insurance company

  - Certain expenses may be excluded from reimbursement

Even though there are a lot of perceived negatives when it comes to traditional long-term care insurance, many couples choose to utilize it given the peace of mind it affords them.

An Alternate Approach: Life Insurance

Some insurance companies offer life insurance policies that have chronic illness benefits that have the same triggers as traditional long-term care insurance. While these policies cover the same types of conditions, the policies themselves have a number of material differences. These include the following:

- Underwriting is based on mortality (life expectancy), not morbidity

- Joint and back problems don't generally figure into the underwriting process

- Premiums may be guaranteed never to rise

- If the insured dies never having needed long-term care, the death benefit can be passed onto heirs

- Benefits are paid based on indemnity (no receipts required), not reimbursement

- Death benefit is given to insured in advance of death, typically 25% at a time over 4 years. This benefit may be discounted at the time of disbursement depending on the age of the insured.

Here's an example of how a life insurance death benefit might be used to pay for long-term care expenses:[34]

- The insured has a $400,000 death benefit

- The insured can no longer perform 2 of 6 activities of daily living

- A doctor writes a letter stating as much

- The insurance company advances 25% of the $400,000 death benefit ($100,000) every year for 4 years (no receipts required).

- The $100,000 annual benefit may be subject to discounting depending on the age of the insured when the chronic illness arises

In short, life insurance is not always the best option when looking to mitigate the cost of long-term care but it can be an alternative that provides flexibility and security that contrasts with some of the more traditional approaches.

---

[34] The hypothetical example is for illustrative purposes only. Each individual's situation or policy is different.

In Summary

Long-term care planning is a critical part of preparing for retirement in the 21st century. A lifetime of savings can be "spent down" in the waning years of one's retirement to pay for the ever-increasing costs of care. The following should be considered in determining how to best mitigate the risk of long-term care:

- A long-term care event may have a devastating impact on your retirement

- Medicaid steps in only after "spend-down"

- The community spouse retains a Minimum Monthly Maintenance Needs Allowance (MMMNA) of around $2,500, one house, one car and up to $120,900 of liquid assets

- There are 4 ways to handle long-term care expenses

    - Self-insure

    - Rely on family

    - Purchase long-term care insurance

    - Use life insurance that doubles as long-term care insurance

Appendix 1

Risk Profile Questionnaire

Please select ONE answer to each of the following questions.

Section One: Financials	Total

1. What is your investment objective?

- ☐ Preserve Principal (0)
- ☐ Income (1)
- ☐ Income and Growth (3)
- ☐ Growth (4)
- ☐ Aggressive Growth (5)

☐

2. What is your current household income?

- ☐ Under $25,000
- ☐ $25,000 - $49,999
- ☐ $50,000 - $99,999
- ☐ $100,000 - $249,999
- ☐ $250,000 - $500,000
- ☐ Over $500,000

3. What is your approximate net worth (excluding your principal residence)?

- ☐ Less than $50K
- ☐ $50K-100K
- ☐ $100K-250K
- ☐ $250K-500K
- ☐ $500K-750K
- ☐ $750K-1.0M
- ☐ $1.0M-1.5M
- ☐ $1.5M-2.0M
- ☐ $2.0M +

4. What is your federal income tax bracket?

- ☐ 10%
- ☐ 15%
- ☐ 25%
- ☐ 28%
- ☐ 33%
- ☐ 35%
- ☐ 39.6%

5. What is your investment experience?

- ☐ None
- ☐ Limited investment experience
- ☐ Moderate investment experience
- ☐ Extensive investment experience

Section Total ☐

Section Two: Time Horizon   Total

1. When do you expect to begin withdrawing money on a regular basis from your investment accounts?

☐ Less than 1 year (1)   ☐ 4-6 years (4)   ☐ More than 10 years (8)   ☐

☐ 1-3 years (2)   ☐ 7-10 years (6)

2. For how many years will you be making the withdrawals?

☐ 1-3 years (1)   ☐ 7-10 years (3)   ☐

☐ 4-6 years (2)   ☐ More than 10 years (4)

Section Total ☐

Section Three: Your Risk Tolerance   Total

1. Indicate the response that you feel best describes your risk tolerance.

☐ Conservative (0)   ☐ Moderate (4)   ☐ Aggressive (8)   ☐

☐ Moderately Conservative (2) ☐ Moderately Aggressive (6)

2. What is your annual investment return expectation relative to inflation?

☐ Satisfied with investments **keeping pace** with inflation. (0)

☐ Prefer investments to **significantly outpace** inflation and am willing to accept moderate long-term risks to achieve this goal. (4)

☐ Desire investments to achieve **highest performance** possible and am willing to accept substantial long-term risk to achieve this goal. (6)

☐

☐ Like investments to **moderately outpace** inflation and am willing to accept some long-term risk to achieve this goal. (2)

3. How strongly do you agree or disagree with the following statement: "I am willing to lose larger sums of money is short term if I can enjoy potentially higher returns in the long-term?"

☐ Strongly agree (5)   ☐ Disagree (1)   ☐

☐ Agree (3)   ☐ Strongly disagree (0)

4. How much do you rely on income from your investments?

☐ Heavily (0)   ☐ Somewhat (2)

☐ Moderately (1)   ☐ Not at all (3)

☐

5. Investment decisions involve a trade-off between risk and return. Risk is any possibility of loss to your portfolio value. Return is the amount earned or profit on an investment. Generally, investments with the highest potential for gains carry the greatest risk of loss. Which hypothetical portfolio are you most comfortable with, considering the possible outcomes of $100,000 invested for 5 years:

Worst Case   **Best Case**

☐ Portfolio 1: $50,000 $300,00 (6)

☐ Portfolio 2: $75,000 $250,000 (4)

☐ Portfolio 3: $100,000 $200,000 (2)

☐ Portfolio 4: $110,000 $150,000 (0)

☐

6. Which statement best describes your investments goals?

☐ Protect the value of my account. In order to minimize the chance of loss, I am willing to accept the lower long-term returns provided by conservative investments. (1)

☐ Balance moderate levels of risk with moderate levels of returns. (3)

☐ Keep risk to a minimum while trying to achieve slightly higher returns than the returns provided by investments that are more conservative. (2)

☐ Maximize long-term investment return. I am willing to accept large and sometimes dramatic fluctuations in the value of my investments. (4)

☐

7. Historically, markets have experienced downturns, both short-term and prolonged, followed by market recoveries. Suppose you owned a well-diversified portfolio that fell by 20% (i.e. $100,000 initial investment would now be worth $80,000) over a short period, consistent with the overall market. Assuming you still have 10 years until you begin withdrawals, how would you react?

☐ I would not change my portfolio (6)

☐ I would wait at least 3 months before changing to options that are more conservative (2)

☐ I would wait at least 1 year before changing to options that are more conservative (4)

☐ I would immediately change to options that are more conservative (0)

☐

8. Which of the following statements best describes your attitude towards long-term investing?

☐ I am willing to accept the lower returns associated with conservative investments that have minimal chance for loss of principal. (1)

☐ In order to pursue moderately high returns, I am willing to accept significant fluctuations in the value of my investments. (5)

☐ In order to pursue moderate returns, I am willing to accept moderate fluctuations in the value of my investments. (3)

☐ In seeking maximum returns, I am willing to accept large fluctuations in the value of my investments and substantial risk of loss to principal. (7)

☐

9. If a unique circumstance were to require an amount of capital equal to at least one-fourth the value of your portfolio, where would you obtain your money?

☐ All from this portfolio (0)

☐ The majority from this portfolio (1)

☐ From other saving/investments (4)

☐ Less than half for this portfolio, and the remainder from other savings and investments (2)

☐

10. Which hypothetical portfolio are you more comfortable with, considering the possible range of returns, for $100,000 invested, over a one-year period?

The percentages for each portfolio reflect the maximum amount that each portfolio may gain or lose in this hypothetical scenario. Note that the portfolio with the highest potential gain also has the largest potential loss.

☐ A (0) ☐ B (1) ☐ C (2) ☐ D (3) ☐ E (4)

$100K

$105K $107K $110K $115K $125K
$102K $100K $95K $90K $75K

☐

11. Describe the kind of risk you are comfortable with:

☐ I could handle being down over a three-year period, but not longer. (3)

☐ I could handle a one-year loss, but do not want to pursue a strategy that could result in longer periods of loss. (2)

☐ I could handle losses over one or two quarters, but would not be comfortable subjecting myself to longer down periods. (1)

☐ I don't want to lose any money ever. I could handle only a very small loss over a few months at most. (0)

☐ I could accept being down over longer than three years if my long-term return potential was above average. (4)

☐

Section Total ☐

Total all Sections ☐

Suggested Investment Mixes

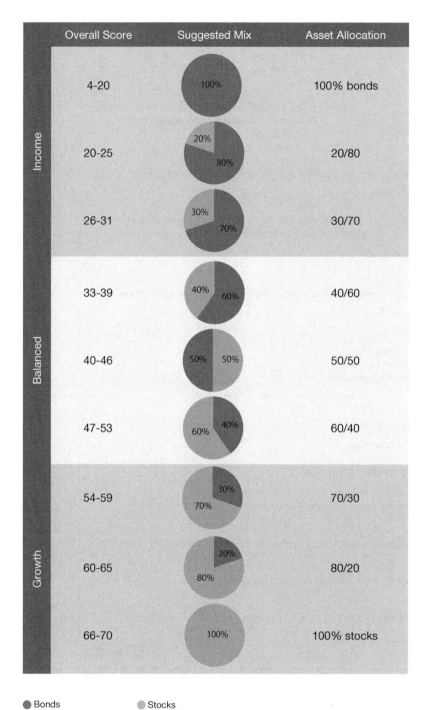

Overall Score	Suggested Mix	Asset Allocation
	Income	
4-20	100%	100% bonds
20-25	20% / 80%	20/80
26-31	30% / 70%	30/70
	Balanced	
33-39	40% / 60%	40/60
40-46	50% / 50%	50/50
47-53	60% / 40%	60/40
	Growth	
54-59	30% / 70%	70/30
60-65	20% / 80%	80/20
66-70	100%	100% stocks

● Bonds   ● Stocks

Made in the USA
Columbia, SC
31 January 2019